A Dose Of

self love

Cosmic Byron

5

A Dose of Self Love

Written by: Cosmic Byron
Illustrated by: Grace Fox

Dedicated to.. ily & xo
two beautiful daughters

 **self-love**

/ˈˌself ˈləv/

1. regard for *one's own well-being and happiness* (chiefly considered as a desirable rather than narcissistic characteristic).

2. *non-negotiable*

also available by Cosmic Byron
The Power of Adversity

NOW

AVAILABLE

Self-Love Declaration

I .... [Insert Name Here]

Declare that it is the uncertainty of what self discovery may reveal, that ultimately frightens many of us into a conditioned state of suppression. I, along with those of the committed collective, acknowledge the fear, but will no longer allow it's generated sensations to paralyze my efforts. I am fully aware that this journey, will come with it's share of difficulties, challenges & set backs, but I refuse to allow that to impede the visceral connection to self. I am on my side & will continue to be, despite what I may encounter along this journey. I shall isolate when needed, resurface only when intrinsically instructed & repeat this process as often as necessary. I am ready to improve the quality of the relationship I have with myself, by any means necessary. I will be selective with the energy I allow into my immediate environment, I will vocalize affirmations filled with a resonance of love & I will express what is inherently ready to be shared with the collective. From today forward, I will no longer look at self love as an act of selfishness, but instead as an act of selflessness.

Sign: .... Date: ....

SELF-DECLARATION

But first love yourself..

because the love of self is *non-negotiable*

But then love yourself..

because the love of self requires no
apologies & comes with no contingencies

But also love yourself..

because the love of self is laced in
forgiveness & dipped in authenticity

often times we're so busy on
the search for love *externally*,
that we simply neglect to
nurture it in the one place
that requires it the most..

...take this moment to celebrate you, even if you aren't where you desire to be. Let go of the societal conditions that confine your expansive thinking, manipulating us into thinking that we have to be this & have to be that. Learn to appreciate this moment & we've just learned to appreciate eternity. Be soft, be gentle & be forgiving. Fall immensely in love with this process & everything about it, including you, even if it's not how you desire it to be. Radiate love & reciprocate it, because love is all that we are.

...the quality of my energy emittance is a priority, not for them, but for myself. I consistently remain grounded, not because it's automatic, but because I consciously implement activity, that yields the result. When I drift, I drift, I don't judge nor criticize the event. It's more of an observance, like let's see where this intrusive thought wants to go. I ride it's wave & when the wave subsides.

I simply return home

you should try putting
yourself first more often &
watch how many things
begin to solve themselves..

Once I aligned,
everything else
worked itself out.
-Cosmic Byron

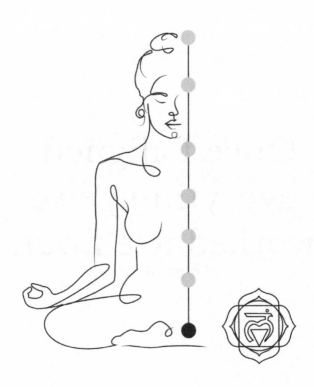

place your palm on your *root chakra,*
& take 3 deep breaths..

...pause for a moment & allow the connection to establish. Slightly apply pressure to the root chakra, acknowledging the presence of your palm, the warmth, the texture & all sensations. Breathe that energy in & exhale any energy that doesn't align with safety, security & confidence. Instinctually, yes we are designed to seek out potential threats in the immediate environment, but right now in this particular moment of time & space, you are safe. So, shift the energy from an external focus to an internal alignment. Envision our most primal & fundamental energy center in a tranquil state. With that vision in mind, whisper affirmations that promote safety, security & confidence. Continue to sit with the self, touch the self & consciously explore the self. *Think Safety*

What words, emotions & sensations come to mind when you hear the phrase *Self-Love*?

_____

_____

_____

_____

_____

_____

_____

_____

_____

_____

_____

_____

_____

_____

_____

_____

_____

_____

_____

_____

_____

Sitting with the perceptual self won't always download into love & light, sometimes isolation requires reaching a depth where light doesn't appear to penetrate. The deeper the exploration, the clearer it becomes that light & dark simply aren't opposed, but actually one in the same.

Rather than suppression, let's create
safe space. Let's create this space
with fluidity in mind, filled with
malleable characteristics to bend &
adjust accordingly to the extension &
expansion of the ever evolving self.

self doubt told me dig the hole, ego told me to dig the deepest hole possible, intuition told me that no hole exist & to put the shovel down..

...let's return home & by home, I'm referring to the internal. Despite the conditions of it's current state, I have the ability to remodel & redesign to my specification. Imagine for second, the possibilities of what can be created in this infinite space. The cultivation of possibility & wonders are limitless. Mistake not for second, this will require immense dedication, but what better to be dedicated to, than to the journey of self love.

deemed *mistakes* aren't a
reason to diminish self
esteem, starve this paradigm
& instead nurture one that
accepts the self in every
transitional phase of life..

Dear *Self..*

...the sensation associated with being outside of my comfort zone, is starting to feel like home. I'm beginning to trust that sensation, that i've mislabeled as anxiety. This sensation is actually excitement towards the infinite possibilities, that the *universe* is slightly nudging me toward.

I trust *you*

i continue to surprise
myself with the level
of unconditional love
i've accessed..

It's ok to say
"I *Love* me"
out loud

-Cosmic Byron

place your palm on your *sacral chakra,*
& take 3 deep breaths..

...the portal of creation & life force. Where
manifestation & pleasure fuse seamlessly. You
can almost feel the electricity of life force
instantly buzz into your finger tips, as your
palm initiates contact with the surface of your
sacral chakra. Motivated by pleasure, aroused
by flow & sustained through creation. Here is
our driving force to experience radiating
sensation, through the empirical & metaphysic
senses. Be here & be here now, because in this
moment, an opportunity of activation has
become available. *Feel* the universe in &
around your existence, this is you & this is
your chakra activated. Remain open to
experiencing this present moment through
your senses. Through this portal, express your
creativity, intuitively dive into the depths &
explore the boundaries of your sensuality.
Intimately trace the origins of the electricity,
ending at their perceived limits. Where you
take this energy from here, is completely
apart of the creation process. *Think Creation*

How would you define *Self-Love*?

_____
_____
_____
_____
_____
_____
_____
_____
_____
_____
_____
_____
_____
_____
_____
_____
_____
_____
_____
_____
_____

it was through losing everything,
that granted me the ability to find
myself; now i have everything..

...a massive energy shift is taking place. Familiar people, places & things are being uprooted & replaced intentionally. Take a moment to breathe this in, these sequential events have already been craved into the script. Resist not what is for you, but instead embrace the unfamiliarity & walk in the direction toward the unknown.

Surrender

it's only in this present moment that
you have the ability to effect change &
by changing your vibrational frequency,
you subsequently change everything..

...it's the lack of our understanding to exactly what darkness is or can provide, that ultimately makes us fear it. Extraordinary transformations occur within these perceptual limits of darkness. Fear not what you're made of, but instead engage the provided elements. The darkest of skies, always create an opportunity for even the dimmer stars to shine bright.

freeing the self of those things that
no longer serve higher order
purpose, was a challenging concept,
so instead i began to love myself in
healthy ways & those challenging
concepts seemed to free themselves..

Detach from the paradigm, that Self *Love* is selfish..

-Cosmic Byron

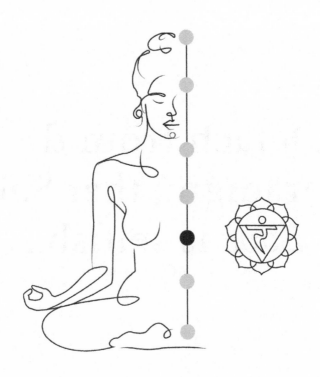

place your palm on your *solar plexus chakra,*
& take 3 deep breaths..

...radiance & personal power illuminate the
external world, when the internal world is in
alignment. Producing healthy self
perception, self-discipline & efficacy, which
are all byproducts of harnessing this
connection of the solar plexus. Envisioning
the potentiality alone, stimulates this region,
mobilizing an electrical current ready &
willing to be utilized in it's boundless ability.
Sit in this moment & envision personal
alignment, manifesting all that you are & all
that you are capable of bringing into
fruition. This forces disengagement in all
forms of "to me" states of consciousness,
allowing space for *oneness* to permeate.
Transmute that disengaged energy into
responsibility, surrender & openness, to
further strengthen the shift into "as me"
state of consciousness. *Think Personal Power*

What are you holding on to that may be impeding a higher connection to the self?

_____
_____
_____
_____
_____
_____
_____
_____
_____
_____
_____
_____
_____
_____
_____
_____
_____
_____
_____
_____

i'm learning to release the applied
pressure, on areas of my life that
require a delicate approach..

softness

go deep
without a need of an outcome

go deeper
without the formation of attachment,
this realm is where the connection is
unconditional, free from judgment &
non-binding

go even deeper
to begin experiencing the liberated self,
in it's truest form

this is freedom

Dear *Universe,*

tear me down,
to build me up
tear me down,
just to build me up again
over & over
for I know this is the process
to true growth..

Sincerely yours

...a beautiful unfoldment occurs when we let go of what could be & embrace what is. Connecting, not attaching, to what is & not what could be. It is the self love in the present moment, not the future that solidifies this connection.

...sit silently, take a moment to witness the thoughts passing before you, just the way they come. Witness them with no added interference or ounce of judgment, because the moment we introduce judgement, we've interfered with the purity. Avoid such labels as *"this is good or this is bad"* these have come from a place of social conditioning & are not pure in universal nature. Sit silently as the energy in thought form passes before you.

observation

Started to realize that I was only feeling what I was supposed to be feeling, exactly when I was supposed to be feeling it. It was never personal, it was just unfoldment.

When the mind is *weak*, the situation becomes an obstruction, forcing the mind & emotion into victim state. When the mind is *strong*, the situation then becomes an opportunity, forcing the mind & emotion into a space of creation.

...happiness is an attitude of the mind. I've learned that the individual defines *his* or *her* happiness. What makes me happy may very well leave you in a state of upset & discontentment. This opens the possibility to create individualized definitions of happiness. We are at our happiest when we are in alignment with *our* core values & beliefs.

when a void is perceived
fill it with love,
although there is no void,
because we are whole,
a little extra love
spread out across the soul,
will never hurt..

The experience
that has pained
you, has come to
nourish you.
-Cosmic Byron

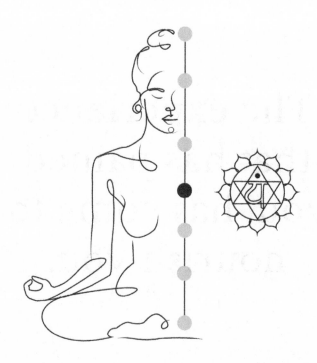

place your palm on your *heart chakra,*
& take 3 deep breaths..

...now feel that expansive energy radiating
within the depths of your existence. This
purge of impurities is being expressed with
intensity. Feel that, breathe that & allow it to
work it's way through you. I am open to
love, let hear you say it. I am open to
forgiveness & I forgive myself, let me also
hear you say that. This vessel is not you, this
vessel is of you, simply a temporary housing
unit, for you to consciously store, explore, &
share your essence. That expansive energy is
you, that expansive energy is love, so when
you think in terms of you. *Think Love*

When was the last time you told yourself
"*I Love You*" and what prompted that moment?

_____

_____

_____

_____

_____

_____

_____

_____

_____

_____

_____

_____

_____

_____

_____

_____

_____

_____

just when you've
thought you've loved
yourself enough, take
another dose..

feel what needs to be felt, learn
what needs to be learnt & from
there we don't reside, but instead
we move forward with wisdom,
experience & love in the heart..

...ride the wave of unconditional
Love towards the self, until the momentum
of the wave is naturally slowed. Allow the
next conscious moment to surface & ride
the wave once again. In this moment, you
will be granted the opportunity to
reinforce the connection & augment the
emittance frequency. It is in the conscious
moment that the emittance frequency of
Self-Love, is at it's strongest.

Be Here

...some days you sit with the self & want to escape as fast as possible. Other days, it's calm & tranquil to be with the self. Then there are the days you sit with the self & are immediately aroused by the energy flowing through you. Whatever the day, allow it; with minimal to no resistance.

Observance

even if they haven't apologized.
forgive them, not for them, *but for you..*

learn how to
love you &
everything
else will fall
into place..

once you learn that
you're enough,
you'll realize that
you've always been..

When all else fails,
continue to *Love*
thy self & a way
will reveal itself..

-Cosmic Byron

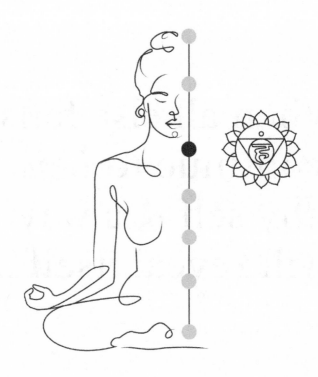

place your palm on your *throat chakra,*
& take 3 deep breaths..

...with your palm in place, gently tighten the grip of your fingertips around your throat chakra, slowly increasing the pressure. Breathe, now release the grip, just as consciously & as slowly as you applied it. Your presence is acknowledged & connection has been restored. Envision your ability to not only understand, but to equally express your inner truth, in an authentic manner. The stronger the vibrational frequency, the more indestructible the connection to esthetic & astral realms become. Feel the arousal of the once subtle & suppressed intuitive abilities, begin to activate. This is the passage way of the combined efforts of each chakra, you've previously established quality connection with. Verbalization whether verbal or non, external or not tend to enter a state of fluidity, when expressing your truth, intra & interpersonally. Listen to & express yourself from higher states of consciousness, while attending to how it resonates with your inner being. *Think Authenticity*

Write yourself a *Love* letter.

_____
_____
_____
_____
_____
_____
_____
_____
_____
_____
_____
_____
_____
_____
_____
_____
_____
_____
_____
_____
_____
_____
_____

...once conscious of *Self Worth*, old habits of settling, now begin to surface. Rather than judgment, we apply compassion & understanding, that those events were simply apart of the awakening process. A continuance of gentle behavioral patterns toward the self, will further strengthen this process on the journey toward *Self Discovery*.

all doors lead to the reflection of
self, here in this moment, is an
opportunity of introspection..

remain present in this moment

even the pieces that seem to
be shattered, are filled with
reflections of perfection..

for many of us, self
love is an act of
reconditioning, an
attempt to re-establish
balance & connect to
the true self..

...there are some people
who are no longer in your
life, that you wanted in your
life, that had absolutely no
business being in your life.
Continue to allow the
universe to work her magic
in & around your existence,
without resistance.

Love is everything,
everything is *Love*..
-Cosmic Byron

place your palm on your *thirdeye chakra,*
& take 3 deep breaths..

...with your fingertips in position, begin to stimulate your ThirdEye in slowed, sensual & circular motion. Focus your attention on the point of stimulation & visualize the chakras' principle purpose of supreme vision. Continue this motion, as the sensations fill with electricity, generating a pulsating current of action potential. Elicit this energy into a state of transcendence, shifting focus beyond optical vision & into an activated clairvoyant ability. The dynamic range of this energy epicenter, is driven by a continuous broadcasting stream of universal consciousness. By deepening our intuitive insight & our capacity to decipher 3D illusion, we enrich not only our worldly perspective, but also the elements of the metaphysical. Consciously access this superior intelligence that governs all things, with no exemptions. The more cognizant we are of this broadcasting stream of consciousness, the more inclined we will be to not only harness it's divinity, but to express it creatively as well.

In this present moment, I am thinking about...

you've outgrown the mold;
you can stop playing small now..

...it's when I lie awake at 3am, that the mind decides to race. These are moments that require I remain gentle with myself. As past regrets creep in, I take 3 deep breaths & witness that same regretful energy begin to diminish. A connection is now restored, the foundation for full acceptance has become available. I must not become attached to this current version, because with evolution comes the natural flow of exchange, so instead I ride the wave of gratitude. As the next version comes forth, I will take 3 deep breaths & with no hesitation, say goodbye to the now expired version.

...at some point you gotta take responsibility & in that moment, is when you'll realize it's been you the entire time. No more shifting, displacing & blaming. *Full responsibility*. In this moment is when you've arrived. Harness the divinity, because your entire existence is now available for cosmic reconstruction, to fit the blue print of your universal purpose.

do not love the self any less in the dark,
but as equally & as unconditionally as
you would in the light..

keep this moment in
my heart, whether good
or bad, it was an
experience none the
less, an experience that
brought perspective &
for that, i will be
forever grateful..

serving purpose

a heart break may be
just what you needed,
to shatter that world
you settled for,
instead of living in a
world you deserved..

keep yourself in situations
that promote progression,
this is one of the highest
forms of *self respect*..

I'm sure they had their reasons, but more importantly, now you have yours. For the distance you're about to implement, but not out of anger, rage or hatred, but from an origin of self love.

with this bomb ass energy,
i understand that i attract
from both ends of the
spectrum, but with this
level of awareness, it
quickly becomes my
responsibility, to only
entertain that in-which i
desire to see manifest..

Become your only source of validation

-Cosmic Byron

place your palm on your *crown chakra,*
& take 3 deep breaths..

...bridging the connection to cosmic-
conscioness, is achieved here at the crown
chakra. Connecting all elements of the
perceived physical, universal consciousness
& spirit, to provide entry into alternative
dimensions & states of consciousness. We're
innately born with the inclination to access
these depths, in a conscious manner. Slow
down & begin to disassociate from
subconscious programming, misinterpretations
& erroneous thinking patterns, all downloaded
from societal based teachings. This will
challenge the perceptual image that we've
developed & accepted, about who & what we
think we are. Doing this, creates the ability to
experience existence through the ever evolving
lens of self activation, where higher self see's
nor experiences separation. That tingling
sensation of electricity is the indicator, that the
portal of enlightenment & self-awareness has
opened. Feel this energy, expand that energy &
allow it to enter, this is the awakening of the
higher self. *Think Enlightenment*

When did I last push the boundaries of my comfort zone?

_____

_____

_____

_____

_____

_____

_____

_____

_____

_____

_____

_____

_____

_____

_____

_____

_____

_____

_____

_____

Take a moment to detox, not just physically, but spiritually & mentally as well. Remain mindful of what you're allowing in & yes, this encompasses people, media & anything else that can potentially affect emotion or even impact the quality of your energy regulation. A conscious mind tends to make the most intuitive decisions.

Unfoldment, not failure..
It was unfoldment, not a failure..
A shift in perspective like this, alters the manner in which we view & process, not just the external world, but the internal as well. This schema in return is directly correlated with the emotional trajectory, we subconsciously subscribe to. Dictating the quality of our emotional response to external & internal stimuli. Unfoldment, not failure. The event rolled out exactly as it was intended to, our resistance to this inevitable fact is what creates the frustration within the emotional human. Detach from control & shift into a space of flow, carving out your purpose like a river through a mountain valley. This process is slow, but proven & remember what ever happens, it's unfoldment, not failure.

the strangest thing occurred
once I ceased to look externally
for completion; realized that i
was already complete..

The Caterpillar in you, has
reached the end of it's journey.
You've crawled a considerable
amount. As beautiful as the
perceived end result, there most
be a process of undergoing
metamorphosis, to even consider
the accessibility to your wings.
Reframe from labels that may
cloud or detour the benefit of such
process. After grounded in a safe
environment, access the shadows,
isolate, shed layers & begin to
digest ineffective aspects of the
old self. Emerge in celebration to
the commencement of this
moment. spread your wings,
admire this victory of overcoming
the self & it is now time to fly.

Transition into what feels good & you know is right, not what you have been conditioned to believe is right. Intuition will always guide & *Love* always has a way in garnering our attention. Answer the tug pulling at your consciousness & explore the desire.

do not feel the fear of falling,
because the same elemental
forces that govern the oceans,
planetary systems & the
smallest particles known to
us, *also govern us..*

that weight is no longer yours
to carry, as if it were ever..

The ability to observe without
reacting, is the result of harnessing
& transmuting energy allocation.
Envision the energy free flowing,
within & surrounding your vessel.
Shift to a state of becoming, because
this is where you consciously raise
vibration to connect with essence of
your existence. Realize that the
energy is you & that you're that
energy. Go in the direction that
serves you & aligns with love.
Harness that energy, that is in
opposition to alignment & love.
Transmute that energy into a higher
vibrational pattern & reallocate it
where it is most required.

Alchemist

Don't be triggered by their actions, especially when you clearly see the open wound. Meet projection with compassion, even if you want to match their aggression with force. Protect your energy & rewire the subconscious to not only be compassionate to them, but more importantly toward the self.

Our nervous system will attempt to signal us when we have entered the space of an energetic force, that does not resonate with our molecular structure. Pay attention to this, because this frequency will attempt to regulate the vibrational pattern, of our cells. Not out of place of superiority, but from a place of self love, immediately remove yourself from the environment & reconnect internally to reestablish molecular balance.

Equanimity

self love is, in a gentle &
loving manner, thinking about
your thoughts & questioning
your mental processes..

On some divine shit, I forgive
you. That doesn't mean I'll
forget, but I also won't allow it
to weigh heavy on my heart.
Whether karma gets you or it
doesn't, is none of my concern. I
had to learn to let what doesn't
serve me go & you were simply
that lesson in the journey.

The level up is for you, not for them. Replace that low vibrational source of energy, with an energy source that radiates high vibrational frequencies.

Consciously create space to allow energy to do it's thing, without meddling. Yes, it'll be uncomfortable momentarily, but the outcome has never failed us. By outcome I'm referring to the resolve, not a snapshot. Often times we confuse a snapshot of the process as the overall outcome & this is the schema that ultimately creates the discontentment, we so often experience.

unconditionally love the self during
every transitional phase of life..

A new day has come
& brought with it an
opportunity of self
forgiveness..
-Cosmic Byron

As you ascend within the context of your journey. The desire to regress & seek comfort in old familiar frequencies, that no longer serve higher order alignment, will be present. Remain conscious durning this process. Look at these expired frequencies with gratitude, as you continue the journey of ascension.

...introspection, is a way to declutter the mind, emotions & rid oneself of thoughts that no longer or have never served as a healthy reference point. When time is taken to be with the self, we are given the opportunity to enhance the quality of connection, we are experiencing within the present moment. Explore the depths & crevices that were once untouched. Fear not what may be revealed, because the contents that have remained suppressed & hidden from the light, have emitted a frequency; self love demands that they be set free. Spread these thoughts, behaviors & beliefs across the table, without the desire to judge or criticize. Filter through each individually, only selecting that which resonates with the soul to be put back. Discard that which doesn't & from here, walk in the profound lightness of this new version, until it is time to shed once again.

it's the energy we must listen to,
not the interpretation of it..

When we operate from a foundation built on self love, the reciprocating elements respond accordingly. Not exactly as we attend, but otherwise accordingly. The focus here is the foundation, establishment, reinforcement & strengthening, through daily self maintenance. Our immediate environment is regulated by a frequency of love, attracting that which is in alignment with love or desiring love. This brings a multitude of energies attempting to connect, according to the nature of & limited to the vibrational frequency of consciousness. You've done the work & have built a foundation on self love, so you respond, not perfectly, but otherwise accordingly. This is your best within the context of the moment & that is all you are required to uphold.

At some point you just get tired of continuously trying to enforce a boundary, that you've respectfully set out of self respect. When this moment arises, reduce frustrations & implement distance, you've respectfully done your part with love & patience.

got to start being ok with allowing them
to think & believe whatever it is they
think & believe, without them offending
or altering your emotional state..

You'll drive yourself insane, attempting to please all people, through the projection of your reality. Embed love & compassion into every action & into every thought. Allow that to be the focus. What they cognitively & emotionally process after that, is on them.

Liberation

step i.. Love thy self
step ii.. Trust intuition
step iii.. Fck their opinions
step iv.. Apply love to step iii

When the state of our energy has become compromised by an external force, our quality of consciousness is momentarily interrupted. Frustration may trickle in, but this energy is not the solution. Allow it to come & allow it go as it came, because it isn't here to remain. When the illusion of smoke clears, allow internal love to reappear. Think not in time intervals, so we can avoid phrases based in how long formats. These are mental & emotional traps. The moment is here & you are in it. Protected, loved & abundant. The storm has cleared & the sea is calm, with your hand on your heart, repeat after me: *I AM STRONG*

Connected to *everything* attached to nothing, is a concept I finally innerstand. Attached to no outcomes, individual, or emotions, simply shifted into a space of flow, allowing what comes to come & what goes to go.

Notes

Notes

Notes